THE BUDDHA'S QUESTION

by W.W. Rowe
Illustrated by Pamlyn Grider

Snow Lion Publications
Ithaca, New York

"Children! I ask each one of you:
What can a simple plume tree do?"

The Buddha sat before a ring
Of puzzled faces. "Anything?

There must be something it can do."
He asked again, but no one knew.

The boys wore silken garments which
Revealed that they were very rich.

The girls — gold bangles on their wrists.
Their saris hung in rainbow twists.

"Children! We all have lived before
And will live many lifetimes more.

We have been animals and plants,
Fish, lizards, birds and even ants.

Perhaps this meeting was prepared
By a past lifetime we all shared.

Once, many thousand years ago,
A little plume tree chanced to grow

Beside a lake. I was that tree.
In crystal waters, I could see

My pale pink blossoms wave and play
When gentle breezes made them sway.

Off to one side, not far away,
A murky, dirty fish pond lay.

In this foul pond lived forty fish
And one fat crab. They had a wish

To swim in water clean and sweet.
It would be such a wondrous treat!

One day, above their heads they heard
The forceful flapping of a bird.

A mighty heron glided down
Beside their pond so foul and brown.

He had a glum and gloomy look.
He shivered, shuddered, trembled, shook.

"Friend heron!" said a trout. "Hello!
Why do you seem to suffer so?"

The heron said: "I'm sad for you.
You float in this disgusting brew

Like pieces of a sea-food stew.
It reeks! It rots! Oh, what a pew!"

"You're right," the trout replied. "It's true.
But there is nothing we can do."

The heron sighed. "That's where you're wrong.
Just look at me. I'm big and strong.

I just flew by a lake so fair,
Its beauty made me stop and stare.

So kindly let me take you there.
Its crystal waters are quite rare."

The fat crab said: "What if this lake
Contains a giant serpent-snake?

Or else, a shark that's long and white
And has a monstrous appetite?"

The heron laughed. "Forget your fright.
You, Crab, must not be very bright.

Serpents and sharks, I guarantee,
Live only in the wide blue sea.

So don't be fools. Just let me take
You to that clear, refreshing lake.

It sparkles. Ah! You will adore
To shimmer downwards and explore

Its cool, sweet depths. And what is more,
A plume tree grows upon its shore."

The trout said: "Even if that's true,
What's in all this, my friend, for you?"

"Dear trout! I'm shocked!" the heron cried.
"You make me suffer deep inside.

I tried so hard today to find
A way to help — and to be kind."

His feathered face grew sad and long.
He sang a mournful little song.

I just wondered (sang the heron)
How you dear, sweet fish were farin'

'Cause I'm such a lovin'-carin'
Always prayin', never swearin'

Never stealin', always sharin'
Always hopin', not despairin'
Ever lovin', carin' heron.
That is what I am declarin'

And I haven't come ascarin'
So you shouldn't be
bewarin'.

The trout had large tears in his eyes.
"Friend heron, I apologize.

Oh, shame on me! I should be cursed.
I trust you now. Please take me first."

With that, he jumped — a silver streak —
Into the heron's waiting beak.

The heron licked a tasty fin
But quickly hid his evil grin.

He gave his mighty wings a shake
And flew the trout straight to the lake.

A short while later they returned.
The trout was tingling. His eyes burned

With sparks of joy and happiness.
"Dear friends!" he cried. "You'll never guess

How beautiful it is! I splashed
Around the lovely lake. I dashed

From shore to shore. It's sweet and clear.
So let's all go — and have no fear.

Let's leave this stinking, steaming stew.
I'll go there now and wait for you."

The other fish splashed their applause.
The trout stayed in the heron's jaws.

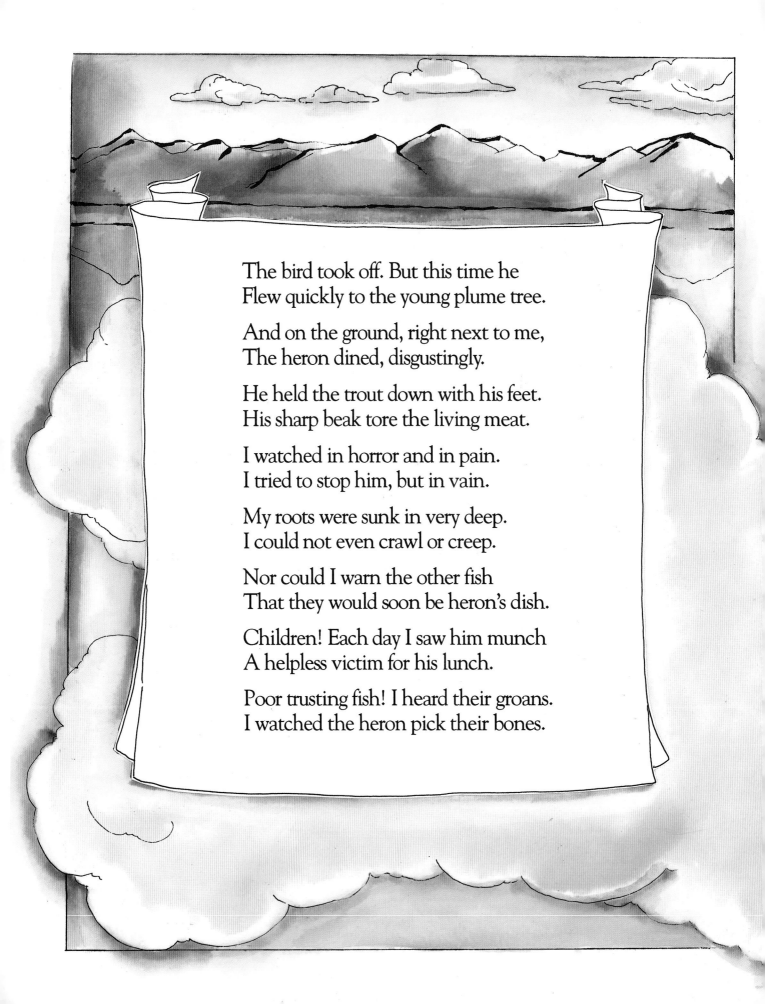

The bird took off. But this time he
Flew quickly to the young plume tree.

And on the ground, right next to me,
The heron dined, disgustingly.

He held the trout down with his feet.
His sharp beak tore the living meat.

I watched in horror and in pain.
I tried to stop him, but in vain.

My roots were sunk in very deep.
I could not even crawl or creep.

Nor could I warn the other fish
That they would soon be heron's dish.

Children! Each day I saw him munch
A helpless victim for his lunch.

Poor trusting fish! I heard their groans.
I watched the heron pick their bones.

My blossoms burst with rage and pain.
From grief, I nearly went insane.

I vowed, in future lives, to seek
Ways to protect the helpless weak.

I felt the victims' dreadful fears.
Pale moisture, in large drops, like tears,

Formed on my bark. But in his glee,
The feasting heron did not see.

The greedy bird ate on and on.
In forty days, the fish were gone.

Beneath my branches, in a mound,
Their picked-clean bones lay on the ground.

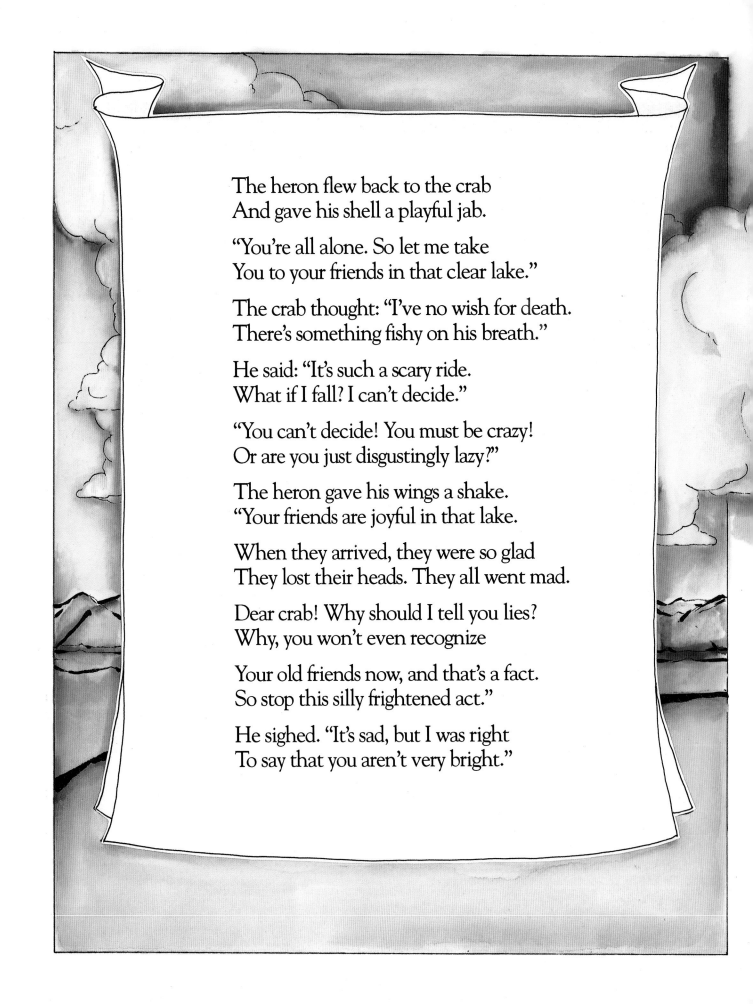

The heron flew back to the crab
And gave his shell a playful jab.

"You're all alone. So let me take
You to your friends in that clear lake."

The crab thought: "I've no wish for death.
There's something fishy on his breath."

He said: "It's such a scary ride.
What if I fall? I can't decide."

"You can't decide! You must be crazy!
Or are you just disgustingly lazy?"

The heron gave his wings a shake.
"Your friends are joyful in that lake.

When they arrived, they were so glad
They lost their heads. They all went mad.

Dear crab! Why should I tell you lies?
Why, you won't even recognize

Your old friends now, and that's a fact.
So stop this silly frightened act."

He sighed. "It's sad, but I was right
To say that you aren't very bright."

The crab replied: "I could be wrong,
But your thin beak does not look strong.

I might slip out. And if I fell,
I'd surely smash and break my shell.

So, to avoid an awful wreck,
I'll wrap my claws around your neck."

The heron shrugged. "All right, friend crab.
But hurry! There's no time for gab."

The crab crawled sideways to the bird.
He climbed aboard without a word

And grabbed the long neck in his claws.
They were as sharp as little saws.

The heron flew straight to the tree.
"You crusty crawly fool!" said he.

"You see that pile of bones? Your shell
Will go on top. Say your farewell."

"You blasted bird!" the fat crab cried.
"You ate my friends! You killed! You lied!

You feathered fiend! You foul disease!"
He gave the heron's neck a squeeze.

The heron squawked and squirmed in pain.
"Dear crab! Friend crab! Let me explain.

It was a joke! A prank! A game!
But now, it seems a little lame.

I shouldn't have attempted to
Deceive a brainy crab like you."

The crab was sadly thinking of
The poor dead friends he used to love.

With all his might, he clenched one claw.
The heron's neck snapped like a straw.

The bird let out a strangled roar.
His head dropped down upon the shore.

It rolled. It stopped. Its glassy eyes
Stared like white marbles at the skies.

The fat crab gave his claws a shake
And disappeared into the lake.

Children! My story now is done.
Perhaps, in that past lifetime, one

Of you was that cruel heron or
A fish who perished near the shore.

And if you like to pinch and grab,
You might have been that clever crab.

But, children, now it is your turn.
Is there a lesson we can learn?"

A hand shot up. "I know! I know!"
A young boy cried from the front row.

"If you are treacherous and cruel,
Yourself is who you mostly fool."

"That's true," the Buddha kindly smiled.
"And when I was that tree, my child,

I saw that if we are cruel now,
It will come back to us somehow.

If we treat others with cruel hate,
That too will be our future fate.

Right then, I vowed I always would
Help other beings all I could

In every future life. And so,
I try to teach you what I know.

Once more, I ask each one of you:
What can a simple plume tree do?"

A small hand waved. "I think I see!"
A young girl cried out happily.

"The vows you made... changed you somehow,
So you can help us all right now!"

"Quite true," the Buddha warmly smiled.
"Your eyes have seen the Path, my child."